BIG FEET, SMALL FEET

Book of Prehistoric Animals for Kids

BABY PROFESSOR

EDUCATION KIDS

Prehistory, meaning before history, is the span of time before recorded history or the invention of writing systems.

Triceratops was a herbivorous dinosaur. The Triceratops is one of the most easily recognizable dinosaurs due to its three horns. fully grown Triceratops were about 8m in length.

Ankylosaurus were one of the last dinosaurs remaining before the large extinction event that occurred. The most recognizable feature of Ankylosaurus was its body armor.

Pterodactyls wingspan could reach up to 40 feet. They were carnivores and probably preyed upon fish and other small animals. Pterodactyls are technically NOT considered dinosaurs.

Tyrannosaurus rex lived throughout what is now western North America. The largest tooth of any carnivorous dinosaur found to this date is that of a T-Rex.

Brachiosaurus is the largest known dinosaur. The length of Brachiosaurus is believed to have been around 26 metres. Brachiosaurus was a herbivore.

Microraptor was a small, four-winged dinosaur. Microraptor were among the most abundant non-avian dinosaurs in their ecosystem.

The name Velociraptor means swift seizer. Velociraptors were bipedal, feathered carnivore with a long tail and an enlarged sickle-shaped claw.